D1364562

UNITED NATIONS

First New Discovery Books Edition 1994

Originally published in Great Britain in 1993
by Exley Publications Ltd, 16 Chalk Hill, Watford,
Herts WD1 4BN, United Kingdom.

Copyright © 1993 Exley Publications
Copyright © 1993 Michael Pollard

All rights reserved. No part of this book may be reproduced or
transmitted in any form or by any means, electronic or mechanical,
including photocopying, recording, or by any information storage
and retrieval system, without permission in writing from the Publisher.

New Discovery Books
Macmillan Publishing Company
866 Third Avenue
New York, NY 10022

Macmillan Publishing Company is part of the
Maxwell Communication Group of Companies.

First Edition
10 9 8 7 6 5 4 3 2 1

Series editor: Helen Exley

Printed and bound by Graficás Reunidas S.A., Madrid, Spain.

Picture Credits: AKG: 11 (top), 12, 15; Associated Press: 21; Exley Publications: 6/7; Gamma: 4, 16, 17 (both),
18, 19, 26, 28, 43, 52 (both), 53 (both), 55, 57, 58, 60 (top); Hulton: 13 (bottom); Image Select: 10; NASA: 60
(bottom); Pictorial Press: 14 (top); Popperfoto: 25, 61; UN: cover, 5, 7, 8 (both), 9, 11 (bottom), 13 (top), 14
(bottom), 22 (both), 23 (both), 29, 30 (both), 31 (all), 33 (top left and right), 34, 35, 38, 39, 44, 45, 46, 47, 49;
UNESCO: 32 (left); WHO: 20, 33 (right bottom), 36 (both), 37, 40/41, 48 (both), 56.

Special thanks to Mohammed Lounes, Gamma Press, Cornelia Visiedo and the UNO for their help.

Library of Congress Cataloging-in-Publication Data
Pollard, Michael, 1931-
    United Nations / by Michael Pollard,
        p.   cm — (Organizations that help the world)
    Includes index.
    ISBN 0-02-726333-9
    1. United Nations. 2. International agencies. I. Title.
II. Series.
JX1977.P615 1994
341.23 — dc20   93-24554
Summary: The history of the United Nations, as well as its impact
on the world today, is described here.

■ ORGANIZATIONS ■
THAT HELP THE WORLD

UNITED NATIONS

by **MICHAEL POLLARD**

New York

ELLENVILLE PUBLIC LIBRARY
40 CENTER STREET
ELLENVILLE NY 12428

Not a single day ...

There are many threats to the welfare of the world's population, and each one is the concern of the United Nations. Some arise from natural causes such as droughts, floods, crop failure, and disease. Others are problems that people create for themselves, such as trading rivalries between nations, injustices felt by one religious or ethnic group compared with another, and oppressive systems of government. And then there is war.

One of the main reasons for the founding of the United Nations was "to save succeeding generations from the scourge of war." In August 1992, there were over fifty-five thousand troops, drawn from the forces of United Nations member countries and wearing the UN's sky-blue helmets or berets, serving in twelve of the world's trouble spots. In the Middle East, UN peacekeeping forces were in Jerusalem, Syria, Lebanon, Iraq, and Kuwait. In Asia, UN personnel were supervising a truce line in Kashmir between India and Pakistan that was first established in 1949, and a large force of twenty thousand troops and advisers was bringing order to postwar chaos in Cambodia. In Africa, there were United Nations forces in Angola, Somalia, and the Western Sahara. In Central America, in El Salvador, UN military observers were keeping a check on human rights and the end of a civil war between rebels and the government. On the Mediterranean island of Cyprus, UN soldiers patrolled the "peace line" between Greek and Turkish Cypriots.

Nowhere are patience and perseverance needed more than in the United Nations' peacekeeping activities. Although there has been no world war since 1945, there has not been a single day when fighting was not going on somewhere. In these one hundred or more "small wars," more people have died than were killed during the six years of World War II.

Opposite and below: Two men with guns, each fiercely believing in their separate cause. Each member of the United Nations peacekeeping force volunteers to save the world from "the scourge of war." It requires a special kind of devotion to duty; they must always respond to violence with calmness and tolerance.

A map of the world. The twelve countries in which the United Nations peacekeeping forces are at work are marked with a blue helmet.

A world family

Keeping the peace is one of the main responsibilities of the United Nations. It is there to keep the forces of disputing nations, or disputing groups within a nation, apart and to give what aid it can to civilians caught in the middle. The United Nations provides a meeting place where issues, and possible solutions, can be discussed. It also provides a channel by which the world's most prosperous nations, such as those of Western Europe and North America, can help the poorer, developing countries that cannot afford to provide adequate food,

Countries with UN Peacekeeping Forces

Areas Served by UN Peacekeeping Forces (12-92)

© Exley Publications Ltd. 1993

Austrian troops of the UN Disengagement Observer Force (UNDOF) supervise the limitation of weapons in Israel and Syria – one of the trouble spots of the world.

water, health services, and education for their people. It also lays down standards for governments to observe toward their peoples, for example in the treatment of political prisoners.

This care for all people is expressed in the United Nations flag, which shows two olive branches — symbols of peace since ancient times — embracing a map of the world. During its history, the UN has experienced many bad times as well as good, but the image on its flag remains as a reminder of the ideals of its founders — that the nations of the world should live in peace and help one another as members of the world family.

"Let us be clear as to what is our ultimate aim. It is not just the negation of war, but the creation of a world of security and freedom, of a world which is governed by justice and the moral law. We desire to assert the preeminence of right over might and the general good against selfish and sectional aims."

Clement Attlee, British prime minister, in 1946

7

Above: Flags of the 179 member states of the United Nations fly in front of the United Nations headquarters in New York City.

Right: Inside the UN headquarters, the Security Council debates the independence of Namibia. When the members are ready to vote, they do so by raising their right arms. The room holds the five permanent members, their assistants, 400 members of the public, and 120 members of the press.

Nation talking to nation

Throughout history, wars have been followed by peace treaties that were supposed to settle disputes between the warring nations. Often these treaties amounted to little more than carving up conquered territory among the victors, without considering the wishes of the people who lived there.

About 150 years ago, the invention of weapons, such as the rifle and the exploding shell, made war more terrifying and more destructive. At the same time, vastly improved communications and the growth of international trade were making the world "a smaller place" with nations more dependent upon one another.

In the nineteenth century, the major European states, which then made up the core of world power, became increasingly aware of their individual "nationhood," increasingly envious of one another, and increasingly prepared to go to war. As the nineteenth century ended and the twentieth began, competition among the European states for territory, trade, and sheer power became fiercer. It exploded, almost without warning, in 1914 with the outbreak of World War I.

The same few hundred yards of land

For four years the European powers and their colonies, followed in 1917 by the United States of America, were locked in a hideous and costly conflict. The fighting was vicious. At sea, submarines callously sank unarmed merchant and passenger ships at the cost of thousands of lives.

In France and Belgium, hundreds of thousands of troops were killed or terribly injured in years of battle after battle over the same few hundred yards of land. But the warring nations pressed on, trying to starve one another into submission by sinking food ships, attacking each other's civilians with aerial and artillery bombardments, and introducing terrible new weapons, such as poison gas, on the battlefield.

Only when Germany and its allies had been defeated in 1918 did the world begin to count the cost. It was horrific. Britain and her colonies had lost well over one million people, including civilians.

France had lost nearly one and half million and

This statue was a gift from the former Soviet Union to the United Nations. It depicts the biblical reference to beating swords into plowshares or turning the weapons of war into the tools of peace. It stands outside the UN building in New York City.

German troops in the trenches on the Western Front in Europe during World War I. When the war began in 1914, troops on all sides joined up enthusiastically. But by 1916 their eagerness had turned to despair as the toll of both military and civilian casualties rose. Three years later, with peace at last in sight, that despair led to the foundation of the League of Nations.

Germany two million. The total number of Russians killed will never be known, but it was certainly more than two and half million.

Apart from this tally of human suffering, the economies of most European countries were in ruins and their people were near starvation. In Russia, the grim toll of war casualties and severe shortages of food and other essentials had provided the spark in 1917 for a revolution that had been threatening for years. In one way or another, the whole world was in a complete state of shock.

The final blow was a worldwide outbreak of a particularly dangerous form of influenza that spread quickly among people living in poor postwar conditions. This epidemic wiped out fifteen million people — more than the total casualty figures of all the warring nations.

Sick of war

When the world's leaders looked back over the devastating years of war, they were at last appalled by what had happened and determined that another similar war should be avoided.

People were not deceived when politicians told them that the dead had "died for freedom." In their hearts, people knew that World War I had been simply a waste of millions of lives. The losers in this war were not only the countries that had been defeated. They were the ordinary families of all nations whose loved ones had been killed or had returned home wounded or with their minds tortured by what they had been through.

Against this background, the president of the United States, Woodrow Wilson, took the lead in suggesting the setting up of a League of Nations. This would aim to help settle disputes between nations, arrange for member countries to help any other member country that was attacked, and eventually, it was hoped, persuade all nations to abandon their weapons of war. The league, with its headquarters in Geneva, Switzerland, started work in 1919.

The league fails

Although some of the league's agencies prospered and live on today as agencies of the United Nations, in its main objective — disarmament and the avoidance of future war — the League of Nations was not successful. It had no forces that it could call on to withstand aggression. Although the league had been largely Wilson's brainchild, the United States refused to join, and for the first years Germany and Russia were refused membership. Its members could rarely agree on what should be done to defuse an international crisis. As for disarmament, the first meeting of the league's Disarmament Conference in 1932 immediately fell apart. France refused to agree to any limits on its armed forces, and Germany, although defeated in World War I, insisted on the right to have forces equal in size to the other powers. The result was that by the mid-1930s, countries were increasing their supply of arms in case of future attack, and aggression had begun to appear again.

Top: The signing at Versailles, France, on June 28, 1919, of the peace treaty ending World War I
Above: The United Nations building in Geneva, Switzerland

11

The league looked on helplessly as first Germany, and then Italy and Japan, began to rebuild their empires by using armed force. The world was caught up in another macabre dance of death and, in 1939, was once more plunged into six years of war.

A new beginning

As World War II drew to a close, plans were again made for another international organization that would make a new attempt to bring nations together.

On June 24, 1945, representatives of fifty-one nations met in San Francisco to sign the United Nations Charter and open a new chapter in international relations. Four months later, the charter came into force and the United Nations was born. Its "birthday," October 24, is still celebrated as United Nations Day.

The charter is the UN's basic rule book. In 111 "articles," or rules, it sets out the aims of the United Nations and describes how they should be carried out. It pledges the peoples of the United Nations to:

— save humanity from the scourge of war;
— protect human rights and the equal rights of men and women and of nations large and small;
— promote justice and respect for international law; and to
— promote social progress, better standards of life, and freedom.

Nations signing the charter agree to be tolerant of other countries, to unite to maintain international peace and security, to avoid the use of armed force, and to work together for better economic and social conditions for all the world's peoples.

Give peace a chance

Diplomats from the fifty-one founding members of the United Nations signed the charter in a mood of great optimism. One diplomat wrote, "After the horrors of the previous six years, a chastened generation of leaders seemed not only to have learned its lesson, but to have agreed on a new system to save succeeding generations

Less than twenty years after the devastation of World War I, known as "The Great War" because no one believed it could happen again, the same horrors were repeated in World War II. Here the people of Germany do their best to continue a "normal" life after the bombing and shelling of Berlin.

from the scourge of war. In this bright new dawn, a world ordered by reason, law and common interest seemed, at last, to be within practical reach."

Twice within fifty years, the world had been ravaged by war, and its people had had enough. It was natural that they should see in the United Nations a new opportunity to give peace a chance.

A dangerous world

The world into which the United Nations was born in 1945 was even more damaged and dangerous than that which saw the creation of the League of Nations. In 1945, two atomic bombs had been dropped on the Japanese cities of Hiroshima and Nagasaki, killing thousands of civilians outright and leaving thousands more to die slowly of radiation sickness and other dreadful diseases.

Developments in the air had been matched by others at sea and on land. Unarmed merchant ships, and even hospital ships evacuating wounded troops, had been mercilessly attacked by submarines and other naval vessels.

One of the most horrific acts during the war, revealed when Germany was conquered, was the systematic murder of millions of Jews, gypsies, and other people whom the Nazi government considered "undesirable." It was not surprising that the United Nations' first concern should be with the preservation of peace and with disarmament.

First priorities

It was a grim picture. And in the closing stages of the war, cracks had begun to appear in the alliance that had defeated Germany, Italy, and Japan. The Soviet Union seemed to be trying to build a Russian empire in Eastern Europe, while the Soviets believed that the United States was trying to expand its influence in Western Europe. The United States alone possessed the most destructive war weapon then devised, the atomic bomb, and was working on even more powerful weapons. Soviet Russia was hurrying to build nuclear bombs. The conflict between the United States and Russia—the two

Below: The picture that haunted the world after August 6, 1945 — the mushroom-shaped cloud created over Hiroshima by the first atomic bomb. Bottom: A victim of the second atomic bomb at Nagasaki, over a year after the explosion.

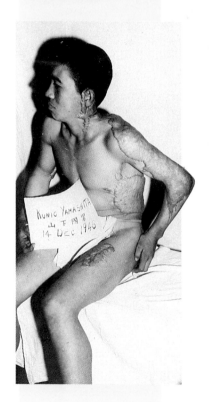

13

"superpowers" — was to develop into what became known as the Cold War, dominated by the threat of each side to use nuclear weapons against the other.

As well as this conflict, there were other urgent and practical postwar problems. The world had almost bankrupted itself during the war. In Europe and Japan, factories had been demolished by bombing. The battles in Europe had been fought over prime farming land that had been largely ruined. Millions of homes had been destroyed by bombing or in ground battles. There was a desperate shortage throughout Europe of food, fuel, housing, raw materials, and manufactured goods.

On top of all this, millions of people had been uprooted by the war from their homes and were now wandering through Europe looking for shelter and work or living in temporary camps. They were joined by survivors from Nazi Germany's concentration camps. Millions more were living in terrible conditions in Europe's cities, often in the cellars of their bombed-out homes or in shelters they had made out of what they could find. With so many people badly fed, poorly housed, poorly clothed, and short of fuel, there was a real fear that, as after World War I, disease would kill many of the war's survivors.

In search of a better life

One of the UN's first acts was to set up an organization, the United Nations Relief and Rehabilitation Administration (UNRRA), to bring immediate aid to the war-stricken areas. Among UNRRA's achievements was the return to their homes of about six million "stateless persons" who had found themselves, at the end of the war, in strange countries without shelter, work, or even any country that they could call their own.

The agency also brought desperately needed food, medical supplies, and other essentials, such as blankets, to the war-torn countries of mainland Europe. Since then, care for refugees has been one of the UN's prime humanitarian tasks, which continues today under the leadership of the Office of the United Nations High Commissioner for Refugees (UNHCR).

UNHCR is one of twenty-one United Nations

agencies that deal with specialized areas of international cooperation. Although these are tied to, and in the end responsible to, the United Nations, they have their own governing bodies and act independently. They have their own headquarters and branch offices in various parts of the world.

There are more than twelve million refugees throughout the world today. UNHCR provides them with immediate help in the form of food, clothing, and temporary shelter.

If refugees want to return home, UNHCR helps both by negotiating with their home governments and with their transportation costs. UNHCR also tries to find new homes for those refugees who do not want to, or are afraid to, return to their own countries.

Opposite top: Dachau, one of the many Nazi concentration camps where six million Jews, gypsies, and "undesirables" were murdered

*Opposite below: The San Francisco Conference
Below: At the end of World War I, there were eleven million refugees in Germany alone: ordinary people who found themselves with no houses, no food, and, often, no family.*

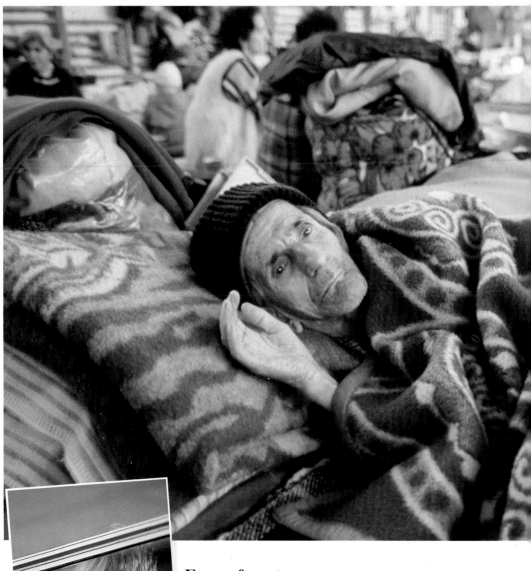

Escape from terror

The work of UNHCR in the civil war in Yugoslavia demonstrates just the kind of role it performs. One evening in August 1992, as the sun was setting, a convoy of buses lumbered into the port of Split on the Adriatic Sea. They were crammed with women, children, and elderly men, weeping with relief after a nightmare 125-mile journey across the mountains from Sarajevo. They were Bosnian Muslim refugees fleeing from the destruction of their homes by Serbian forces taking part in the civil war in what had,

Above and opposite: Following the breakup of Yugoslavia, Serbian troops attacked Muslims in Bosnia-Herzegovina. The suffering people of this war-torn country, both old and young, looked to the United Nations peacekeeping forces to transport them away from danger, to give them food and blankets, and to try to stop the war.

until a year before, been Yugoslavia. The country was now torn apart by racial and religious strife, and the refugees were among the war's innocent victims.

The long day had begun at dawn in Sarajevo. There, the refugees had made their tearful farewells to relatives they were leaving behind and climbed aboard the line of buses, taking with them the few possessions they could carry. When the buses were full, a United Nations personnel carrier, bearing the blue-and-white UN flag, took up position at the head of the line. Another followed at the rear.

17

Borislava, Anja, and baby Stanko

The convoy moved off with its UN escort to shepherd it through the dangerous streets of the city, where mortar shells and sniper fire might start flying at any moment. But the journey to the outskirts went smoothly. There, the UN escort stopped, and the buses proceeded on their own. They had been promised a safe journey — but after months of fighting in Sarajevo, it was hard for the refugees to believe that they would not be attacked or the buses blown up by mines in the road. Borislava Karadglaja, who was on the bus with her two children — eight-year-old Anja and baby Stanko — said, "I was all the time expecting gunfire or something to explode around us."

Borislava had left her husband, mother, and father behind in Sarajevo. "I came to bring my children out of that hell," she said. Another passenger on the bus, Katica Icic, had been unable to face life in Sarajevo any longer. Three weeks before, her mother had been killed when a shell exploded beside her while she was out shopping. Then Katica's home had been wrecked, and with her husband she had had to find refuge in a crowded cellar. Now, with her baby, Nerma, and her cat, Katica had fled, leaving her husband, Farouk, behind to fight.

On to a new life

At Split, the refugees' journey was not over. They were to travel by ferry up the coast to another port, Rijeka, where the UN had set up a temporary camp for them and other Muslim refugees from the fighting. There, they would try to recover their shattered nerves and start to prepare for a new life. Perhaps they would be offered a home in one of the western European countries that had agreed to give the Bosnian refugees a fresh start.

Borislava, Katica, and their children were among three hundred Bosnian Muslims evacuated from Sarajevo that day — just a small group among thousands of people fleeing from their homes in war-torn Bosnia. The help they received from the United Nations in escorting them from the city and providing temporary shelter at the end of their journey was only a tiny part of the worldwide effort made by the UN to prevent war and, if it cannot do that, to protect its victims.

Opposite: Relief supplies arrive at Sarajevo airport under UN supervision.

Below: The role of UN peacekeepers is to remain impartial and avoid taking sides in the disputes they are policing.

Above: Children in Burkina Faso, West Africa, greet members of a UN agency team. But too many of the world's children (opposite) still cling precariously to life.

Caring for children

Another UN agency is the United Nations Children's Fund, UNICEF. This also began as an emergency organization after World War II, when children in Europe and China were suffering as a result of shortages of food, clothes, and medicines. Then UNICEF turned its attention to longer-term needs of children in developing countries. Among the projects it funds are well-drilling for clean water, helping with the repair of schools, and training local people in child care. At the same time, UNICEF also brings relief to children and families caught up in civil strife, epidemics of disease, or natural disasters.

The General Assembly

The heart of the United Nations, and the focal point of what is called the United Nations "family," is based at the UN headquarters in New York. The work of the United Nations is carried out by six bodies that were set up under the charter. Each body has its own duties.

The General Assembly is where world issues are debated in an annual session that runs from September to December. Each member country in the United Nations can have up to five representatives, but only one vote, in the assembly. Subjects, or "resolutions," to be discussed by the assembly are suggested by committees of members that sift through the ideas put forward and choose what they think are the most urgent and important ones. On the most vital issues, such as questions of peace and security, the vote must show a two-thirds majority. With over 150 languages represented at the United Nations, delegates and members of staff communicate with one another through six "official" languages — Arabic, Chinese, English, French, Russian, and Spanish.

When speeches are made in the assembly, where any national language may be used, skilled translators provide simultaneous translations that delegates can hear through headphones. Documents are translated into the six official languages. In its daily work, the Secretariat uses English and French.

Below left: Pope John Paul II addressing the UN General Assembly during his visit to the United States in 1979

Below right: In the General Assembly, Mother Teresa, winner of the 1979 Nobel Peace Prize, attends the premiere of a documentary of her work in India. The secretary-general in 1985, Javier Perez de Cuellar, is to the left.

Drawbacks ...

It is not hard to find fault with the UN General Assembly. One former member of the United Nations staff once described it as a "preposterous and repetitive bore."

It has no power. It cannot make law in the way that a national government can. The national representatives who attend and vote represent the governments, not the peoples, of their countries. They are not elected by their peoples, and the governments that appoint them may not have been democratically elected themselves. And whatever views the General Assembly may express, the countries involved can ignore those views if they wish, and there is nothing that the assembly can do about it.

Every member has a right to speak, so debates can drag on for hours, often with the same points being made over and over again by different speakers. No wonder that some people regard the assembly as merely a "word factory." But, as Winston Churchill is reported to have said, " Jaw-jaw is better than war-war." Many debates in the assembly attract only small attendances. There is a United Nations joke about a delegate who found himself speaking to an empty hall, except for one other diplomat. At the end of his speech, the delegate thanked the one member of his audience for being there. "Not at all," said the listener. "I am the next speaker."

Below left: A tense moment during the Security Council debate in 1974 on the future of Cyprus. The Mediterranean island has been divided since 1974 into two separate communities, Greek and Turkish. UN efforts to solve the problems this causes have, so far, been unsuccessful.
Below: Six official languages are used in the UN General Assembly. Speeches are translated into these languages by teams of interpreters working in the gallery, which can be seen on the far wall. Their translations reach delegates through headsets.

"The UN has a seemingly
limitless capacity to
produce often lengthy
documents in six
languages and in immense
quantities. Efforts to
eliminate a document
usually provoke a group of
governments to demand its
continued existence, and
other governments will
probably support them in
case they wish to exert a
similar privilege in the
future."

Brian Urquhart, former
undersecretary general of
the UN, 1987

...and benefits

But criticism of the assembly is not entirely fair. For many smaller countries, it provides an opportunity for the world to hear about the particular concerns of their peoples, perhaps on a question of health or food supply or the threats posed by the activities of other countries. In this way, it alerts more powerful and influential nations to possible future threats to peace, or perhaps to issues of human rights.

It is also worth remembering that a small country, such as Papua New Guinea or Malta, has the same vote in the General Assembly, and the same right to speak on an issue, as a major world power like the United States. For small countries that also have an interest in world affairs, the assembly offers a rare chance for their voices to be heard, however briefly, on the world stage and on important world issues.

The world's watchdog

The second body central to the work of the United Nations—and particularly to its peacekeeping role—is the Security Council.

The council's powers are different from those of other parts of the UN organization, which can only make recommendations to governments. The Security Council can make decisions that governments *must* accept and carry out, or risk penalties, such as economic sanctions—restrictions on trade with other countries—or even, at worst, expulsion from membership.

From the start, the powers of the Security Council were designed to avoid the main problem of the League of Nations—that the peacemaking efforts depended on all members accepting its views. The more people who meet around the table in a committee, the less chance there is of their being able to agree. So the size of the Security Council is limited to five permanent members (China, France, Russia, the United Kingdom, and the United States) and ten nonpermanent members who serve for two years and are elected by the General Assembly.

The five permanent members were the alliance that had won World War II. In 1945, they were the world's

"The UN...can never be
anything but a mirror
of the world as it is. It
merely assembles together
the multiplicity of
individual nation
states with all their
imperfections.... It is
no use blaming the UN,
therefore, for deficiencies
which are those of the
world it reflects. The
UN is as good or bad as
the nations which
compose it."

Evan Luard, former British
delegate to the UN, 1979

leading powers and had the world's largest armed forces. As the Security Council was given the right to use military force to keep the peace, it made sense that the world's most powerful nations should have permanent seats.

But what if the five permanent members could not agree on the use of military force? The situation might then become dangerous, and this was the reason for the introduction of a special voting rule in the Security Council, the rule of the veto. A Security Council resolution can go ahead only if none of the five permanent members votes against it.

Problems again

When the United Nations was founded, it was taken for granted that the five nations—China, France, the Soviet Union, the United Kingdom, and the United States — that had united in war would continue to do so in peacetime. But it soon became clear that the five nations' wartime cooperation was over.

One problem was the Soviet Union, whose Communist system of government was very different from that of its partners. It had suffered most during the war and was anxious to preserve peace. But the method it chose was to occupy large areas of Eastern Europe and so build a safety zone between itself and the West.

The other problem was China. During the war, in order to defeat Japan, the two rival political parties in China, the Nationalists and the Communists, had united under the leadership of the Nationalist Chiang Kai-Shek. It was Chiang's Nationalist government that was represented on the Security Council. But when the war was over, the Communists restarted their fight for power in China. In 1949, Chiang retreated with his government to the offshore island of Taiwan, and a new Communist government was proclaimed in mainland China. Up to 1971 the Nationalists still had their seat on the Security Council, representing the fourteen million people of Taiwan, while mainland China, the nation with the world's largest population of over seven hundred million, was not represented.

It was evident that the Security Council was going to run into more big problems. Two days after its first

Chiang Kai-Shek, a Nationalist who claimed to represent the entire Chinese population in the UN Security Council. Communist China eventually got a permanent seat on the Security Council in 1971.

A heavily armed Palestinian guerrilla fighter. The dispute over Israel has dominated world politics since 1948, when the state of Israel was declared by the Security Council. The UN has been trying to keep peace there through three wars and countless guerrilla activities, as well as kidnapping and terrorism.

meeting in January 1946, Iran complained to the council that its security was threatened by Soviet troops who had remained in the country at the end of the war.

The Soviet Union replied by pointing out that there were still British troops in Greece and Indonesia. Then Syria and Lebanon complained about French and British troops on their soil. The peace-loving words that had greeted the foundation of the United Nations were fading.

Two more serious threats to world peace — which were to last for fifty years — were brought to the Security Council.

The Middle East

After World War I, Palestine — the "Holy Land" — had been designated as a national home for the Jewish people, much to the anger of the Arabs, who formed the majority of people living there.

In 1947, the problem was brought to the United Nations Security Council, and a plan was made to divide the area into Jewish and Arab sectors. In May 1948, the new Jewish state of Israel was proclaimed, and on the same day it was attacked by the combined armies of five Arab states.

The Security Council sent in negotiators and military observers, and from that day on, through two more wars and countless threats of others, the Arab-Israeli dispute has never been far from the headlines or from the attention of the UN. It has proved to be one of the most difficult of the world's problems.

The second long-running dispute to come before the Security Council concerned another area of land poised between two groups with opposing religious beliefs. This was Kashmir, one of the states of what had been British India. When Britain gave India and Pakistan their independence in 1947, both countries claimed Kashmir as part of their territory.

The state's Hindu leader had chosen to join India, although the population was mainly Muslim and would have preferred to be part of Muslim Pakistan. After outbreaks of fighting along the Kashmir border in 1948, a team of military observers was sent in to police a cease-fire — and it is still there.

In fact, most of the disputes in which the UN has

become involved through the Security Council are still unsettled. Despite this, UN peacekeeping forces have either prevented most of them from escalating into full-scale war or have kept a fragile peace settlement in place.

But the expense of peacekeeping is a drain on the purses of all UN members, and this has led some world leaders to call for more negotiation between disputing nations and less direct UN action. It is too easy, they say, for nations to make threatening noises at each other, and even take threatening action, in the knowledge that "the UN will sort it out." Other diplomats see this idea as a return to the days of the League of Nations, when the league could only talk while nations fought.

Meanwhile, the Security Council acts as a kind of fuse, preventing the outbreak of wars that could drag in other nations and threaten the peace of the rest of the world.

Paying for the United Nations

Responsibility for carrying out the recommendations of the General Assembly and the resolutions of the Security Council is the work of the third central UN body, the United Nations Secretariat. This is a kind of international civil service made up of permanent officials and their supporting staff, drawn from member nations.

The UN employs about five thousand people to carry out its day-to-day work at the UN building in New York, and another 10,500 in offices around the world. In addition, the many agencies of the UN employ another thirty-five thousand people, the majority of them experts in such fields as economics, sociology, agriculture, health, physics, nutrition, banking, and translation.

These people also include experts who join UN agencies for short periods to train people or to take part in a particular project. This might be, for example, a plan to develop improved techniques of fishing in a country dependent upon its fishing industry or one for setting up prenatal care clinics for pregnant mothers in a country that lacks such facilities.

The cost of running the United Nations and its specialized agencies is met almost entirely by the governments of member countries, and to a smaller extent by private individuals.

"To remain calm in the face of provocation, to maintain composure when under attack, the United Nations troops, officers and soldiers alike, must show a special kind of courage, one that is more difficult to come by than the ordinary kind. Our United Nations troops have been put to the test and have emerged triumphant."

Javier Perez de Cuellar, UN secretary-general 1982-1991

Above: The UN headquarters in New York is the hub of the United Nations Department of Public Information. The department produces publications, films, and videos about the organization's work and also services the world's broadcasting media with radio and television relays of General Assembly and Security Council debates.

The UN's "regular budget" — that is, its normal day-to-day running costs — is met by assessments of each member country's ability to pay. This means that the wealthier countries pay more and the poorer countries less. The United States, as the world's richest country, pays one-quarter of the UN's regular budget, while there are seventy-eight developing countries that are assessed to pay only 0.01 percent each. But these figures can be deceptive. For example, Gambia, a developing country that pays the minimum, still contributes a higher percentage of its national income than any other country.

One of the problems about United Nations funding is that some countries pay late or refuse to pay part of their contribution altogether. They withhold payments that are to be used for purposes they do not approve of. Some have used the principle of nonintervention of the UN in a member country's internal affairs as an excuse not to pay. The result is that, although many people believe that the UN is an extravagant organization, it is usually fighting very hard to keep its essential services for peace and humanity going.

The regular budget accounts for only about one-third of total UN expenditure. The rest is raised by voluntary contributions from member states. Some of the agencies of the United Nations family — the United Nations Capital Development Fund (UNCDF), the United Nations High Commissioner for Refugees (UNHCR), and the United Nations International Children's Fund (UNICEF), for example — depend entirely on voluntary contributions, from governments, national organizations, and even from individual people.

The late American oil billionaire, John D. Rockefeller, gave the UN the land on which its New York headquarters were built. Each year millions of people help the United Nations International Children's Fund by buying UNICEF greeting cards.

The face of the UN

At the head of the secretariat, the United Nations' third main body, is the secretary-general, the UN's top permanent official, who is appointed by the General Assembly. The secretary-general comes into the public eye most often as a peacemaker, flying around the world to try to bring disputing states together to settle their differences.

The secretary-general's job is difficult, but vitally important. Impartiality in disputes involving member nations is crucial, and there must be no suspicion of better treatment being given to one side than to the other. For this reason, the six secretaries-general so far have been from countries that have nothing to do with the superpowers and that are not likely to be involved in disputes themselves. Most have served for ten years, except for the first, the Norwegian diplomat Trygve Lie, who resigned in 1953, and his successor, Dag Hammarskjöld of Sweden, who was killed in a plane crash while in office, also having been secretary-general for eight years. The sixth secretary-general, Boutros Boutros-Ghali — the first African to hold the post — took office in 1991.

Members of the secretariat staff are employees of the United Nations, but they are, of course, still citizens of their own countries. This could lay them open to conflicts of loyalties in their everyday work. To avoid

Above: The UN maintains a worldwide communications network by satellite, linking the New York headquarters with other offices and field operations around the globe.

"The secretary-general is in a way the eyes, the ears, the mind, the heart and the voice of humanity."

Robert Muller, former UN assistant secretary-general

29

"All in all, the International Court of Justice, with all its limitations, represents one of the most effective of the organs of the UN, and is some ways the one with the greatest potential for the future."

John Ferguson, from
Not Them But Us

this, they all take an oath promising to serve the interests of the United Nations as a whole and not to accept instructions or influence from their own national governments. "What is expected of the United Nations staff members," says the UN, "is impartiality and determination to act in the interest of the organization rather than that of any particular country. Whatever their own personal or national preferences, staff members must avoid letting their own feelings stand in the way of this trust."

Making world law

As well as the General Assembly, the Security Council, and the secretariat, the three other central bodies of the United Nations are the International Court of Justice, the Trusteeship Council, and the Economic and Social Council (ECOSOC).

The International Court of Justice, based at The Hague in the Netherlands, took over the functions and buildings of the "World Court" established in 1920 by the League of Nations. The court consists of fifteen judges, each drawn from a different member nation of the UN. Nations in dispute over matters of international law can take their cases to the court, normally just referred to as "The Hague."

Subjects coming up before the court vary widely from a border dispute between El Salvador and Honduras in Central America to protests from Australia and New Zealand over French testing of nuclear weapons in the Pacific Ocean.

Below: UNTAG was a UN peacekeeping operation designed to help the African state of Namibia gain independence. After many disappointments, an agreement was signed under UNTAG auspices in 1988. This promised Namibia independence by at least mid-1991.
Below right: Under UN supervision, votes are counted in the vital referendum that was held to decide Namibia's future.

In most cases, the decision of the International Court of Justice has been accepted by the disputing nations, although there is no way in which it can enforce its findings. For example, in 1984 Nicaragua complained to the court that the United States was interfering in its internal affairs. The court found the complaint justified, but the United States refused to abide by the decision or even to accept that Nicaragua's protest should have been made to the court!

Unfinished business

The Trusteeship Council is the smallest of the constituent bodies of the United Nations set up under the charter in 1945, and it is a strange one since its purpose is to work itself out of a job. The two world wars left a number of territories that were former colonies of the defeated nations. When peace came, they had no real government.

In 1945 Britain, France, and the United States agreed to look after these eleven territories until they were able to govern themselves. The largest was Tanganyika, which before World War I had been a German colony and since 1918 had been administered by Britain. Tanganyika became independent in 1961 and three years later merged with the island of Zanzibar to form the Republic of Tanzania.

When the trust territories, as they are called, become independent, the UN Trusteeship Council plays no further part in their administration, so the council will eventually disappear.

Above: A UN supervisor checks the arrival of ballot boxes in the Namibian referendum. Below left: The president of South Africa, F.W. de Klerk, shaking hands with the leader of the new independent state of Namibia, Sam Nujoma, at the granting of independence in 1990. Below right: The celebration of independence for Namibia. The UN has been most successful in helping many countries making a peaceful transition from colony to independent state.

Above: The United Nations Educational, Scientific and Cultural Organization (UNESCO) saved the 3,250-year-old Abu Simbel temple in Egypt from destruction by flooding from the Aswan High Dam in 1968.

Above right: World Health Organization (WHO) workers spray waterways to kill malaria-carrying mosquitoes in the Philippines.

Making better lives

In the United Nations Charter, members pledged themselves to "promote higher standards of living, full employment and conditions of economic and social progress and development." They promised to seek solutions to international economic, social, health, and related problems, and to promote universal respect for human rights and freedom regardless of race, sex, language, or religion.

These activities are the responsibility of the UN's Economic and Social Council (ECOSOC), which coordinates the work of the United Nations "family" of specialized agencies, such as the World Health Organization (WHO) and United Nations Educational, Scientific and Cultural Organization (UNESCO). ECOSOC operates through a network of special commissions for particular topics or areas of the world, for example the UN Commission on Narcotic Drugs and the Economic Commission for Africa.

One word sums up most of the work of ECOSOC and its committees and agencies: development. We live in a

world full of inequalities. Its wealth is concentrated mainly in the developed world also known as "the North": North America, western Europe, the oil-rich states of the Middle East, Australia, and Japan. In these countries, one-third of the world's population lives in relative comfort. The poorest areas include central Africa, parts of Southeast Asia, and also pockets of poverty in Central and South America and the Caribbean — the developing countries or "the South." Here, two-thirds of the world's population fights a continuing battle against poverty, hunger, ignorance, and disease.

Poverty does not mean merely not having enough money to buy everything the developing countries want. It means not having enough to provide people with essentials such as sufficient food, shelter, health care, work, and education. The first aim of the development work carried out by ECOSOC and its network of organizations is to try to relieve the immediate suffering of people in the developing countries. The second is to improve the developing countries' economies so that eventually they will be able to raise their standards of living by their own efforts.

Above left: Dams provide irrigation and also power for domestic use and manufacturing industry. This dam is part of a UN aid project in Indonesia.
Above top and above: The WHO, a UN agency, makes the provision of a clean water supply a priority for both livestock and people.

This scene at a garbage dump in Manila in the Philippines is repeated in many of the world's largest cities. People lured to the city in search of work have to fight for survival in any way they can. Agencies within the UN's Economic and Social Council (ECOSOC) battle hard against these degrading conditions.
Right: Survival was beyond these victims of the drought in the Sahel region of Africa, hit by decades of crop failure. WHO figures estimate that 210 million people in the world suffer from extreme malnutrition.

Imbalance in our world

The problems of the developing countries stem from a number of causes. Some of the countries are in areas where the climate is unpredictable or the soil poor, which makes farming difficult and uncertain. Some are in areas vulnerable to natural disasters, such as earthquakes, floods, or sudden drought. Bangladesh is already devastatingly poor and overpopulated, and thousands of square miles of farmed land is flooded each year. Others have few natural resources that they can export in return for goods from the developed world.

After World War II, some developing countries were not sufficiently prepared for self-government. Internal political struggles and, in some cases, civil war drained what little economic strength they had. In others, real or imagined threats from surrounding countries led to heavy spending on arms instead of on essentials such as health, education, housing, and agriculture.

Most developing countries depend for their income on the export of raw materials like timber or metal ores,

34

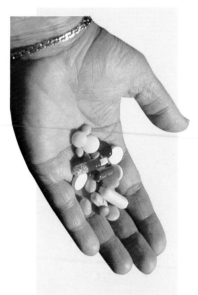

or cash crops such as coffee, rice, and cotton. This makes them vulnerable to the demands of the developed world, which may demand lower prices, and to economic changes resulting from political decisions. One example of this is what happened to the Caribbean island of Jamaica, whose major export is cane sugar. In the 1970s the European Community decided on a policy of cutting back on imports of cane sugar in order to help European farmers who produce beet sugar. The result was an economic crisis in Jamaica, which, in turn, produced political violence.

Measuring poverty

There are many ways of measuring conditions in poorer countries, but all of them show a dramatic contrast with life in the developed, industrialized world. For example, in Japan, western Europe, and the United States, life expectancy is, on average, seventy-five. In Afghanistan, one of the developing countries, it is only thirty-seven, and in Ethiopia, it is forty-two.

Another way of measuring poverty is to count the number of babies who die in the first year of life. In Afghanistan, one in five babies does not survive until its first birthday. In the United States, the number of babies who die under one year old is less than three out of every thousand.

As for food, an intake of about 2,330 calories per day is regarded by nutrition experts as the average daily requirement for most people. This is exceeded in many developed countries. However, in Bangladesh, the average calorie intake is less than two-thirds of what is needed for good health.

A further indicator of poverty is the availability of clean water. Many fatal diseases, such as cholera and dysentery, are spread by germs that are carried in impure water. It has been estimated that over one-quarter of the world's population cannot obtain safe water for its everyday needs.

In health care, also, the difference between developed and developing countries is huge. In Britain, there is one doctor for every eight hundred people. In the African state of Burkina Faso, there is one doctor for every fifty-six thousand people.

Drugs available cheaply in the developed world (above) can cure many prevalent tropical diseases, such as river blindness (below).

Closing the gap

These contrasts add up to an enormous world problem that the Economic and Social Council (ECOSOC) and its agencies have tried to tackle in a number of ways. First, there are the practical steps that agencies, like the World Health Organization (WHO) and the Food and Agriculture Organization (FAO), can take, such as programs for immunization, for the provision of safe water supplies, and to teach farmers better working methods. Many such programs are funded with United Nations money, which it obtains from member countries, and have been spectacularly successful. In 1980, WHO was able to announce the complete eradication from the whole world of a disfiguring and often fatal disease: smallpox. But these programs can only nibble at the edges of the worldwide problem of inequality between rich and poor nations.

ECOSOC also works to convince the United Nations' richer member nations of the importance of narrowing the gap: by contributing money, personnel, and equipment to projects in the developing nations, but more importantly by organizing the world's economy so that the developing countries get a fairer share of global wealth.

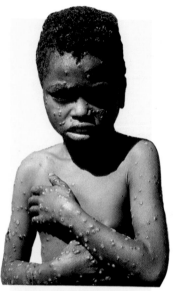

Above: A victim of smallpox showing the painful sores of this fatal disease. It is now part of the world's medical history.

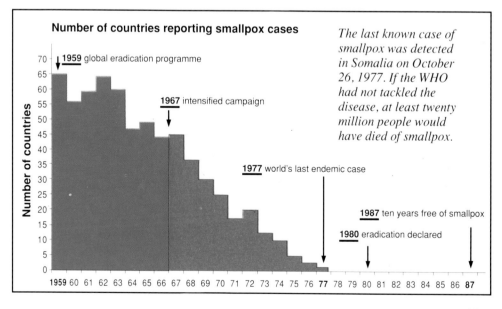

Number of countries reporting smallpox cases

Number of countries

70 — ↓ **1959** global eradication programme
65
60
55 — **1967** intensified campaign
50 ↓
45
40
35 — **1977** world's last endemic case
30
25
20 — **1987** ten years free of smallpox
15
10 — **1980** eradication declared
5
0

1959 60 61 62 63 64 65 66 67 68 69 70 71 72 73 74 75 76 **77** 78 79 80 81 82 83 84 85 86 **87**

The last known case of smallpox was detected in Somalia on October 26, 1977. If the WHO had not tackled the disease, at least twenty million people would have died of smallpox.

*"The United Nations
and the specialized
agencies do things on
an altogether new
scale. They maintain
military forces,
undertake emergency
tasks of civilian
administration, lend
and invest, survey
resources and purvey
know-how ... and help
governments to feed,
teach, heal and train,
modernize farming
methods, disinfect crops
and food reserves,
improve nutrition,
eradicate malaria and
operate airports and
radio communications;
and they do most of
these things, and many
more, on a large and
increasing scale."*
Dr. Wilfrid Jenks, from
The World Beyond the
Charter, *1970*

*Below: Training given
by UN volunteers and
staff in basic skills, such
as motor mechanics,
enhances economic
independence in
developing countries.*

One way this can be done is to distribute manufacturing industry more widely. Encouraging the growth of industries is an important aspect of development. The developing countries are major suppliers of fuels and raw materials, usually at very low prices. The industrialized world benefits from the employment and profits created by using these raw materials and fuels to manufacture goods, some of which are exported back to the developing world at prices it finds hard to pay. If more manufacturing were done in the developing countries, their economies and employment figures would benefit, and they would be able to earn more foreign currency by exporting goods at higher values.

One country where this problem has been tackled successfully is Indonesia in Southeast Asia, where timber is a major product. At one time almost all of this was exported as a raw material, to be made into plywood, chipboard, and other timber products in the industrialized world. In the 1980s, the Indonesian government, with help from the United Nations Industrial Development Organization, embarked on a plan to improve the national economy. Part of the plan was to encourage manufacturing. As a result, timber products from the country's own raw material are now made inside Indonesia, providing both work and increased income from exports.

Money and skills

The UN's development work, performed by ECOSOC and its agencies, includes providing money from international sources for various development programs. One of these sources is another UN agency, the World Bank. The agencies also send teams of experts, such as doctors, veterinarians, agricultural specialists, and teachers, to the poorer countries to pass on their skills to the local populations.

At UN headquarters, ECOSOC works to persuade the industrialized nations of the need for more investment and more commitment if the problems in the rest of the world are to be overcome.

In Africa, the International Development Association (IDA), a UN agency, provided funds to the republic of

Togo to finance improved cotton and food crops, to Mali for improved grazing, seed production, and crop protection, to Benin for seeds, insecticides, and fertilizers, and for improved water supplies in Niger.

In Asia, the IDA made a loan to China to help fund a program for agricultural education, and to Burma to build two dams to provide irrigation and clean drinking water to dry areas. It funded a program for over ten thousand wells and water supply systems in rural areas of the Philippines. It also lent Malaysia the money to support a plan to plant new strains of high-yielding rubber and fruit trees for small farmers and to irrigate their rice fields. In Korea, a World Bank loan helped to improve rural roads and so reduce the costs of getting crops to market. In Western Samoa, a loan funded a project to help small farmers improve pig, goat, and poultry production.

In Morocco, the World Bank provided a loan to enable small farmers, livestock producers, and forestry workers to increase their productivity. Other World Bank loans helped to pay for agricultural education in Tunisia and an irrigation project in Cyprus. The IDA provided funds for small farmers in the Yemen Arab Republic to buy seeds and tools.

In South America, Peru received a World Bank loan to help rebuild its national agricultural university after earthquake damage, and another to help new settlers in a rural area establish their farms.

All these projects took place over a two-month period in 1983. Development is not just a matter of providing seeds and equipment. It also involves developing a country's farming skills and knowledge and training experts who will eventually be able to guide a developing country's agricultural future, providing food for tomorrow as well as today.

Above: In many poor countries, economic progress is held back by the shortage of energy supplies. With the backing of UN experts, many countries are exploring new energy technologies. This example, from Kenya, is a plant that generates power using geothermal heat from deep inside the earth's crust.

Just one meal a day

But for some developing countries, farming will never bring prosperity. Nepal, for example, is one of the world's poorest countries, dependent almost entirely on farming. Set in the foothills of the Himalayas, to the north of India, only about one-fifth of its land area is suitable for farming, and most of this is in the south of the country.

Two-thirds of Nepal's population live in the hills, eking out a fragile existence on poor, often steeply sloping soil.

The Thapa family are typical hill farmers. The Thapas are a large, extended family consisting of Bahadur Thapa, his wife and six children, his parents, and his brother's wife and children — fifteen people in all. They have less than 2½ acres of land from which to feed themselves, mainly on rice and vegetables. The Thapa family lives from day to day, fighting for survival. Often, their normal two meals a day are reduced to one, and sometimes they have to go without food altogether for a day or more. For fuel, the Thapas depend on wood gathered from the nearby shrinking forests.

The only way that the Thapas and families like them can obtain money is by sending their young men south across the border to India to work on farms there. Some

In Nepal, a hill farmer with a pair of oxen works land that is about the most difficult in the world to farm. The terrain is sloping, the soil of poor quality, and the climate unpredictable and often violent. UN development work in the southern region of Terai attempts to ease the conditions of these hill farmers.

settle in India and never return. Meanwhile, deprived of some of their most active and useful family members, the hill families find it even harder to farm.

Monsoon country

Countries like Nepal present the greatest challenges to the UN development planners. Floods and landslides following monsoon rains can ruin the work of years by carrying away irrigation channels, together with the growing crops. Heavy monsoons in 1983, according to a UN official, destroyed twenty years of development work within three days. The effects of the monsoons are made worse by the gradual depletion of the forests. When trees are cut down, the soil beneath them becomes unstable and easily washed away. Yet Nepalese hill farmers like the Thapas have no other source of fuel for cooking and heating.

With its mountains and deep valleys, Nepal is ideal country for hydroelectric power, produced by gathering, storing, and then releasing the monsoon rains through water turbines. But the cost of building power stations and lines to carry electricity to the farms is far beyond what Nepal could afford — and most of the population is too poor to be able to pay electricity bills.

Most of the UN's development work in Nepal has been in the southern region of Terai. Here, for nearly twenty years, the International Development Association has been funding an ambitious irrigation project that has multiplied the food production — and the incomes — of Terai family farmers by three times. Good news — but the increased prosperity of Terai has resulted in the movement of hill farmers southward in search of a better living. The narrow strip of fertile and well-irrigated land can only support a limited population, and so development, while helping with one problem, has created a new one.

"It is not true that there is insufficient food to go round. The grain produced, if properly distributed, would give every human being ample protein and more than 3000 calories a day. But a third of the grain produced is fed to animals. There are terrifying anomalies. In 1971 during acute drought the countries of the Sahel actually exported 15 million kilos of vegetables, mainly to Europe. In 1974, after the floods in Bangladesh, people could not afford the rice which was actually available."

John Ferguson, from
Not Them but Us

The darker side of development

Back in 1945, it seemed possible that the United Nations would be able to lead the world on a steady march to the point where there was no poverty. This was the hope contained in the United Nations Charter — but sadly, it proved to be too optimistic.

Despite the efforts of the agencies, backed up by aid from individual countries and backbreaking work by some of the developing countries, the majority of the world's population is still underfed, deprived of adequate health care, and living in poor conditions. Progress in defeating world poverty has been painfully slow.

Part of the reason for this is the size of the gap between rich and poor countries. This calls for huge investment that has not been forthcoming. However much the United Nations, as a world organization, urges that more money should be made available for aid to developing countries, it is dependent upon the governments of member countries for aid funds. Some governments prefer to channel their own aid packages direct to the poorer countries, sometimes in the hope that this will buy them political loyalty. Others donate as little as possible, especially when times are hard in their own countries.

The UN family of agencies is permanently short of money. The result is that a great deal of aid has to be in the form of loans that the countries must pay back with interest. This burden of debt, in turn, adds to the problems of the poorest nations.

Talk, talk, talk

In 1960, the UN announced the start of a Development Decade with the object of making a serious fresh start on the problem of development.

There were many discussions and conferences, but so little was actually achieved that it was decided to call the 1970s the Second Development Decade and, eventually, the 1980s the Third.

In 1974, the General Assembly approved a "New International Economic Order." This committed the UN to making it possible to "eliminate the widening gap between the developed and the developing countries." Other plans and strategies followed in an increasing flood, mostly studying the problems of development

The flight of people from the country to the cities in search of work is a problem in most developing countries. The result is that cities become overcrowded and the new arrivals have to build their own homes where they can, out of whatever they can find. Poor living conditions like these in New Delhi, India, lead inevitably to extremely bad health, crime, and other social problems.

*"If the Governments
cannot agree to feed the
world, they cannot
agree about anything."*
    Boyd Orr

*Opposite: Even in
normal times, the people
of Uganda eat, on
average, between 10%
and 15% less food than
they need. This leaves
them vulnerable to
disease and, if there is a
crop failure, to the quick
onset of famine. Does the
UN do too much talking?*

*Below: The Sahel is a
strip of land along the
southern edge of the
Sahara Desert in Africa.
The combination of
twenty-five years of
drought and the
overgrazing of the
sparse vegetation by
stock animals has caused
the desert to spread
southward, resulting in
starvation and death for
herdsmen, their families,
and their animals.*

without actually doing much about them. There was no shortage of good intentions, expressed on mountains of paper. But the poorer countries, in urgent need of aid, not words, could not be blamed for regarding the UN's professed concern as mere talk.

Talk could not prevent a single child from dying. It could not produce enough food for a single family. It did not sink wells or dig irrigation channels to produce better crops. It did not provide medical care for families that had never seen a doctor in their lives. Most important of all, talk did nothing to bring the worst-off out of their terrifying poverty.

Crisis in Africa

This desperate contrast between talk and action was exposed sharply in 1985. A crisis, which had been developing for years in eastern Africa, suddenly burst upon the world's conscience — even though experts had been warning of it long beforehand. The Sahara Desert was expanding because of changes in the climate and poor farming methods, bringing drought and famine to Ethiopia and Somalia. The crisis was made worse by civil war and by a rapidly growing population — resulting in one of the greatest human disasters in history.

In 1985 and 1986, despite humanitarian aid from the United Nations and from individual countries and relief organizations, over one million people died of starvation. Television pictures of the victims horrified people all over the world.

In the middle of all this came a startling piece of news. The UN General Assembly had decided, by 122 votes to 5, to spend $73 million in Ethiopia. Not on food for the starving. Not on housing for the millions who were fleeing the drought areas. The money was to be spent on a new conference complex in Ethiopia's capital, Addis Ababa, to house the UN's Economic Commission for Africa. The commission's communications system, it was reported in an official UN publication, was outdated and "other facilities were in serious need of repair."

The $73 million would, critics of the UN pointed out, have brought hope to millions of Ethiopians who were in "serious need" of food to stay alive.

The Green Revolution

Some United Nations aid programs are badly managed and inefficient, and others — as with the Addis Ababa conference complex — are aimed at the wrong targets. But others, although successful, can still misfire like the so-called Green Revolution — an effort to improve the productivity of farming in the developing countries with the object of helping them to feed themselves.

The Green Revolution was extremely successful in carrying out this aim. Between 1950 and 1985 the area of the world's land made fertile by irrigation doubled. It also introduced new and more productive strains of cereal seed that produced up to ten times as much grain. Combined with the use of artificial fertilizers and pesticides, use of these new seeds increased world cereal production by two and a half times between 1950 and the late 1980s. China and India, two countries that had previously had to import grain, were able by 1990 to grow enough of their own.

This was a success story — but it had another side. In developing countries most farmers are poor, working small plots of land with the help of their families, often using hand tools. They could not afford the new seed or the chemical fertilizers and pesticides, and their farms were too small to make the use of agricultural machinery worthwhile, even if they could have afforded it. The result was that while the farmers with large areas of land prospered, many poor farmers lost out. They had to sell their land to wealthier farmers and go to work for them for low wages. Others simply sold out and went to the cities to look for work.

The success of the Green Revolution contained two conflicting messages. It certainly resulted in better crops and less hunger. But it also had less desirable economic and social effects. The United Nations and its agencies learned their lesson, and in recent years more emphasis has been placed on agricultural development projects aimed at small farmers.

Development aid is such a complicated issue that it is easy for developed countries, which do not want to take part, to find reasons why they should not. In democracies, national budgets are examined closely by voters who know that they will be paid for out of taxes,

Below: Pesticides can increase farm production — but they can also be a menace to wildlife. This duck was the victim of pesticide use in the Netherlands. The chemical leached into its freshwater habitat.

and soon questions are asked about the aid that is sent to developing countries.

Is the money being well spent? Not always; some of it goes for government palaces and such luxuries as sports complexes and conference halls. Does the money reach the people in need? Not always; there is a great deal of corruption in some developing countries that siphons off aid into the pockets of politicians and officials or to feed the army. The result is that it becomes increasingly difficult for the governments of developed countries to persuade their people of the need to reduce the world gap between rich and poor.

Above: Farmers in the United States and other developed countries can afford expensive equipment to pump water from below ground to irrigate their crops. This option is not available in the developing world. There, farmers cannot afford the equipment, and in many places there is no source of water.

Out of sight, out of mind?

Attitudes in the industrialized world to developing countries also depend on what is in the news. Coverage in newspapers and on television of, for example, a famine may produce pressure to send aid. But when some new topic pushes the story out of the headlines, even though the crisis has not been solved, aid tends to dry up.

It is also easier to attract aid for the victims of some sudden natural disaster than for the less spectacular and

Below: One of the World Health Organization's success stories has been the steady fight against malaria, spread by mosquitoes that breed in swamps. The WHO's effort is two-pronged. Swamps are sprayed to kill the mosquitoes, and drugs are distributed to treat malaria victims. Bottom: In the 1980s, a new threat to world health emerged with the identification of AIDS, caused by the HIV virus. Here, a Ugandan AIDS victim is mourned.

longer-lasting work of building up a developing country's ability to look after its own people adequately.

The difficulty of obtaining development funds from the richer countries increased when, during the 1980s, the first signs of recession appeared in the developed world and it, therefore, became more concerned with the survival of its own economic and social systems. Even in the grip of recession, with unemployment levels rising and average incomes falling, people in the developed countries were still incomparably better off than those in the poorer countries, but this was a difficult message for the United Nations to get across.

The UN's development work through ECOSOC comes in for a good deal of criticism. It often seems that the more prosperous UN members are happy to talk endlessly about the problems of the developing world but less eager to contribute to solving them.

More commitment, please

Despite the good and effective work done by the UN agencies in the field, if there is to be real progress all the UN members will have to commit themselves more fully to that aim.

But, as a former British United Nations delegate has written, "it is a pity that operations to find homes for millions of refugees, to bring rapid emergency relief after grave natural disasters in any part of the globe, to wipe out smallpox from the earth, to stamp out the drug trade all over the world, to help organize family planning activities among much of the world's population, to organize the world's meteorological services, or abolish pollution in the oceans, to mention only a few, are not so well known to the general public as the angry speeches hurled across the horseshoe table of the Security Council chamber."

Disarming the world

World disarmament — reducing the size of national armed forces to the level needed only for a country to defend itself — is a major aim of the United Nations. It was also the main objective of the League of Nations.

The league believed that if nations built huge military forces armed with the latest and most horrific weapons, it was inevitable that one day these would be used. The experience of World War I had proved the point.

However, in the 1930s countries began to rearm again, resulting in World War II. By 1945, weapons of war had become even more deadly and destructive — so destructive as to threaten the whole future of the earth. The UN saw disarmament as an even more urgent issue.

The threat to the survival of civilization is not the only reason for promoting disarmament. The manufacture of weapons and the maintenance of large armed forces costs nations money that could be better spent in other ways, such as improved health services, education, and other peaceful objectives.

A report published in 1980 pointed out that one-half of one percent of the world's military expenditure in one year would provide all the farm equipment needed to enable *all* the needy countries in the world to feed themselves.

To marchers like these, protesting against the arms race, the UN's steps to get world disarmament have seemed painfully slow.

"Every time you create more sophisticated weapons you are forcing countries in a war situation to keep up with the others in military hardware. This compels them to continue buying more and more sophisticated weapons. One should bear in mind that there are two parties in the trade in arms."

*Susata de Alwis, former
Sri Lankan ambassador to the UN*

World War III?

What dominated the thinking of the founders of the United Nations in 1945 was, however, sheer terror. During World War II, the United States had developed the atomic bombs that were then dropped on Japan. These marked a whole new lurch forward in the ability of humankind to destroy itself.

One atomic bomb, dropped by one aircraft, could devastate a city. It was not fully appreciated at the time that, unlike bombs using conventional explosives, the damage did not stop when the smoke had drifted away. Atomic bombs — and the even more deadly weapons, hydrogen bombs, on which scientists were working — left behind a residue of radioactivity in the atmosphere, on the ground, and in the sea that could wipe out life on earth.

The United States was not the only nation that knew how to produce nuclear weapons. If Germany had not been defeated in time, it would almost certainly have had its own. The Soviet Union quickly caught up with the West after 1945, and the United States, Britain, and France were all competing with the Soviet Union to produce even more devastating weapons and even more efficient ways of delivering them to their targets.

By the mid-1950s, there were many distinguished world figures — the British philosopher and mathematician Bertrand Russell and the American scientist Linus Pauling were just two — who doubted whether the world would survive to the year 2000 without blowing itself to pieces.

Closer and closer

As the years went on, these fears seemed to be confirmed by what everyone could see each night on television news. In 1961, East Germany, with the support of the Soviet Union, built a wall across the divided city of Berlin, marking the border between Eastern Europe, dominated by the Soviet Union, and the West. Its purpose was to prevent people escaping from poverty-stricken East Germany to the more prosperous West. Any East Germans who were caught trying to cross the wall were shot.

But the Berlin Wall broke the 1945 agreement on the occupation of Berlin that had been signed by the United States, the Soviet Union, Britain, and France. For several tense weeks, United States and Soviet tanks faced each other across the Berlin Wall. Any miscalculation by a tank commander on either side could have sparked off World War III.

While Berlin looked like becoming the flashpoint for a new world war, another crisis blew up. In 1959, the revolutionary leader Fidel Castro had gained control of the government of Cuba, only a short distance away from the southern coast of the United States. He had taken power from a cruel and corrupt dictator, who had been supported by the United States, and he turned to the Soviet Union for economic and military help. In 1962, the United States discovered that the Soviet Union was planning to use Cuba as a base for nuclear missiles that could have destroyed most of the major North American cities.

The U.S. Navy mounted a blockade to prevent Soviet

October 1962, and a U.S. warship challenges a Russian freighter en route to Cuba. The Russian convoy turned back. If it had not, the U.S. Navy would have opened fire — and all the aims and work of the UN would have been futile: World War III would have begun.

ships carrying missile equipment from reaching Cuba, and the American president, John F. Kennedy, demanded that the Soviet Union should remove any weapons that had already arrived. For a week, the world held its breath. At the last moment, the Soviet ships turned back, an agreement was reached, and the danger of war was averted — but the world had been within days, maybe hours, of destruction.

Top and above: The rise of militarism and the emergence of nuclear weapons are the targets of the United Nations disarmament plans. But they have not been successful. People are still marching for peace.

The turning point

By 1959, there had been only one actual disarmament treaty. UN members had agreed to keep weapons out of the Antarctic. As no one lives in the Antarctic, apart from visiting teams of scientists, and no country had shown any great interest in occupying it, this meant very little — except that it showed that agreement *could* be reached on questions of disarmament.

But the events of 1961 and 1962 in Berlin and Cuba persuaded world leaders that the realities of the threat of war must be faced, and led to an increase in the UN's efforts toward disarmament. By 1963, the United States

Above and left: A parade of weapons in the former Soviet Union and a demonstration for peace. The Cold War, fought between the Soviet Union and the United States, raged for over forty years. The UN Conference on Disarmament negotiated for an end to the arms war, each country trying to beat the number and skill of weapons the other side had. Finally, the Cold War ended through discussions held by American president Ronald Reagan and Soviet leader Mikhail Gorbachev.

53

and the then Soviet Union agreed to ban tests of nuclear weapons in the atmosphere, outer space, and underwater (though not underground). They were later joined by the two other countries that had nuclear weapons, China and France.

This was an important breakthrough. For the first time, the major world powers were acting in response to overwhelming world opinion.

Both the United States and the Soviet Union had been carrying out large numbers of atmospheric tests for several years. As a result, the amount of radioactivity in the atmosphere was reaching dangerous levels, increasing the risk of cancer and of radiation damage to the world's population and to unborn children.

Disappointment

The 1963 agreement encouraged further efforts. In 1967, UN members decided not to use outer space as a base for weapons. Other treaties followed — on the spread of nuclear weapons technology to other nations, on the use of biological weapons and poison gas, on establishing parts of the world, such as the South Pacific, as nuclear-free zones, and on banning the use of the seabed as a base for nuclear weapons.

Despite all this, the United Nations' efforts at disarmament have been a disappointment. The really important agreements on arms control, such as the Strategic Arms Limitation Talks (SALT) and Strategic Arms Reduction Talks (START) agreements, were reached between the United States and the Soviet Union alone. The UN had no part in them, except for encouraging them from the sidelines.

The United Nations' own Nuclear Non-Proliferation Treaty of 1968, which aimed to prevent more countries from acquiring the technology to develop nuclear weapons, was signed by most United Nations members but not, significantly, by Argentina, Brazil, India, Israel, Pakistan, and South Africa. All these countries had the ability to develop such weapons and may since have done so.

In an effort to spur its members to greater efforts, the UN declared that the 1970s should be a "Disarmament Decade," aimed at stopping the nuclear arms race and

"They [UN troops] are in essence a non-violent force in a violent situation. Their task is to avoid adding to the sum of violence. They are not empowered to intervene militarily if fighting breaks out between the two parties to the conflict. They lack — deliberately — the equipment or numbers to stop a major military action by military counter-action. They are the voice of conscience, which was once cynically defined as the uncomfortable feeling that someone may be looking. They are the instrument of world public opinion."

John Ferguson, from
Not Them but Us

beginning the elimination of nuclear weapons altogether, along with other weapons of mass destruction. There was a great deal of talk in the General Assembly, but by 1976 the UN had to admit that, so far, the Disarmament Decade had not succeeded.

A special conference was organized. The UN's Disarmament Commission, which had not met since 1965, was revived, with each UN member having a seat on it. A new forty-nation Commission on Disarmament was set up. Ever hopeful, the General Assembly decided to declare the 1980s the Second Disarmament Decade. There was another special conference.

But good intentions, special conferences, and new committees were not enough to overcome what the UN later admitted were "the deeply held national and regional concerns of the member states."

Below: Victims of Iraqi gas attacks on the Kurdish people within Iraq's own borders in 1988. The attacks, in which four thousand Kurds were murdered, aroused worldwide condemnation. The UN Conference on Disarmament tried to prohibit the use of chemical weapons, but, in the end, the UN is only as effective as its members are cooperative.

Opposite: A UN inspector checks a factory in Iraq where it is suspected that chemical weapons are being manufactured, despite Iraqi assurances to the United Nations that it is complying with its regulations.

Below: The World Health Organization was quick to respond when it became clear in the early 1980s that AIDS posed a new threat to the world's population. This poster was part of an international campaign to alert people to the danger.

Will the world ever disarm?

Sadly, it has to be said that in the achievement of even the beginnings of world disarmament, the United Nations has, up to now, failed.

That the world is a safer place today than it was during the early 1960s, when the United States and the Soviet Union seemed to be competing with each other in a race toward the destruction of civilization, is due almost entirely to the efforts of those two countries, acting together without the help of the United Nations. However, the more ominous side to the picture is provided by many developing countries, which have used aid from overseas — especially from the United States, the former Soviet Union, France, and Britain — to build large, well-equipped armed forces far beyond their need to defend themselves. A further worry is the increase in the number of unofficial armies — guerrilla forces — trying to overthrow established governments in southeastern Europe, Africa, the Middle East, and Asia. Through the international arms trade, these forces have been able to obtain modern weapons.

No UN pleas for disarmament are going to have any effect on them, and no one has any real idea of how well armed they are.

But there is one small, encouraging sign. When the United Nations was founded, the armed forces department of most governments was called the War Department. Today, most governments call it the Defense Department. This just might be an indication that governments know the way they *should* be thinking, even if, for the moment, they stick to the outdated idea that "might is right."

Take some credit

But there is a bright side to the United Nations story. There has been no world war during the life of the UN. Since 1945, no country has dropped a nuclear bomb on another country. The terrible hazards of nuclear war have so far been avoided. To universal condemnation, only one country, Iraq, has used poison gas. Space, which could have become a kind of storehouse for nuclear weapons, has been kept free of armaments.

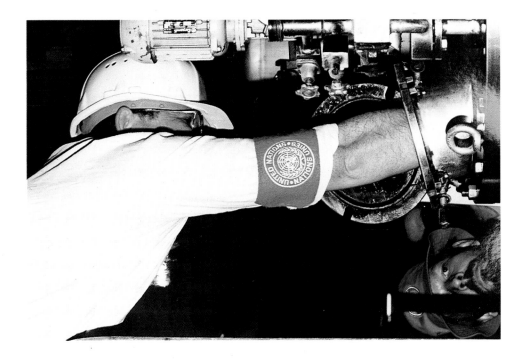

The United Nations can take some of the credit for this. It may have too many committees, and debates in the General Assembly and the Security Council may be noisy, showy, and long-winded, but the fact that the UN is there, and that the actions of its members can be held up and examined, is a constant reminder of the main reason why it was founded — "to save succeeding generations from the scourge of war." And if war does break out between two nations, the UN is there to act as a mediator, separating the opposing sides and trying to bring them to an agreement. The UNHCR will also be there to provide temporary shelter and transportation to refugees made homeless by war, famine, and other disasters. The United Nations Children's Fund (UNICEF) provides health care, food, and education for the children of developing countries. The UN Commission on Human Rights lays down and monitors standards by which governments should treat their peoples. The World Health Organization (WHO) is working on a global program trying to combat AIDS. It estimates that more than five million people in the world may be infected, and the only real weapon against the

Without WHO there would be no global collection of information on communicable diseases, no comparable health or disease statistics, no international standards or guidelines for safe food, or for biological and pharmaceutical products, no evaluation of the cancer-producing risks of pollutants, no global advocacy for healthy ways of life, no international pharmacopoeia, and no universally accepted guidance for global control of the AIDS pandemic.

From a WHO leaflet

disease is prevention. Approximately $100 million goes to almost every country in the world, with one thousand consultants training, treating, and educating people.

An important, active role

The United Nations has also taken an important, active role in the international fight against environmental damage. In 1992, the United Nations Environmental Program (UNEP) summoned a "United Conference on the Human Environment." It became known as the "Earth Summit" and was held in Rio de Janeiro, Brazil. The conference dealt with the problem of nuclear waste, the dumping of toxic waste, the destruction of the rain forests, global warming, and the damage to the ozone layer.

The United Nations Declaration of Human Rights, first drafted in 1948, continues its fight for freedom for all regardless of race, sex, language, or religion. The Declaration was engineered by Eleanor Roosevelt. It was a unique achievement, in that forty-eight countries voted yes to the Declaration, no country opposed it, and eight abstained. Eleanor Roosevelt worked patiently on the document, word by word, for two years to smooth over each tiny disagreement that came from the fifty-six different countries involved.

The Declaration brings the attention of the world down to individuals in a physical, political, and social way. It investigates allegations of torture, of prevention of the freedom of speech, of poor conditions in the workplace, and many more abuses of human rights. There can be few issues affecting human survival and happiness that are not watched over by a member of the United Nations family.

In the field of development, the UN can point to many successes. It has not succeeded in eliminating world poverty, but it has brought relief from undernourishment to many millions of people in the developing countries and saved many more, by providing vaccination and treatment, from fatal or disfiguring diseases.

It has delivered many small farmers in developing countries from the hopeless task of trying to produce food in poor, unirrigated soil, or from raising flocks of

"The Declaration [of human rights] is a magnificent document. It is eloquent, lucid and has coloured all subsequent thought on human rights, by setting down a moral framework that no one since has quite been able to ignore. Its ideals are as relevant today as they were in 1948."

Caroline Moorehead, *from* The Independent, *on the 40th anniversary of the Declaration*

Opposite: UN peacekeepers on patrol. Despite criticisms of the UN, it is the only organization trying to manage the problems of the world by uniting individual nations. As Dag Hammarskjöld, secretary-general from 1953 to 1961, said, " It is an attempt to provide us with a framework inside which it is possible to serve the world by serving our nation, and serve our nation by serving the world."

Above: The caring arm of the United Nations — a vital attempt to prevent war, ensure human rights to all, and promote social progress.

Below: The UN's basic message is that we all live in one world and must learn to share it — or perish.

livestock riddled with parasites and disease. It has helped many countries to take the first steps on the long climb out of poverty.

The changing world

Today, some of the aims of the United Nations Charter seem out of date and hopelessly optimistic. They were written at a time when the world was recovering from a global war that had left few communities untouched. The world — and our understanding of it — has changed, and the United Nations has had to change with it.

Some problems — for example, smallpox — have been eliminated. New ones, such as what to do about environmental pollution, have been recognized. The greatest threat to the world for more than forty years, nuclear war, has receded.

What is certain is that the United Nations is as vital to the world now as it was in 1945. The problems that the world faces are different, but they are problems that can only be overcome by international action. With all its faults, the United Nations is one organization that tries to bring the world's people together peacefully.

Important Dates

1918   Nov. 11: An armistice is signed and World War I fighting stops.

1919   Jan. 20: American President Woodrow Wilson prepares the League of Nations.
June 28: The Treaty of Versailles is signed, bringing World War I to an end.

1920   Jan. 10: The League of Nations officially comes into being.

1931   Ignoring League of Nations' protests, Japan invades China.

1936   Germany, under Adolf Hitler, takes over the Rhineland on its western frontier.

1937   Germany invades Austria and, a year later, Czechoslovakia.

1939   Germany invades Poland with Soviet cooperation.
Sept. 3: World War II starts when Britain and France declare war on Germany.

1941   Dec. 7: Japan attacks the U.S. fleet at Pearl Harbor, bringing America into the war.

1945   May 8: Victory over Germany and Italy is declared in Europe.
June 24: Fifty-one nations sign the United Nations' Charter in San Francisco.
Aug. 6: The United States drops an atomic bomb on Hiroshima, Japan, followed by another, three days later, on Nagasaki.
Aug. 14: Japan surrenders, ending World War II.
Oct. 24: The UN Charter comes into force.

1946   Jan. 17: The UN Security Council meets for the first time.
Feb. 1: Trygve Lie is appointed as the UN's first secretary-general.

1948   May 15: The first Arab-Israeli war starts.
June: UN observers are sent to supervise an Arab-Israeli truce.

1949   Jan.: UN military observers are sent to supervise a cease-fire in Kashmir.
Oct. 1: A Communist government is formed in China, with the Nationalists fleeing to Formosa, now Taiwan.

1950   June 25: The North Korean army invades South Korea.
July 7: UN forces join in the Korean war.

1953   Mar.: Dag Hammarskjöld of Sweden takes over as UN secretary-general.

July 27: An armistice is signed in Korea.

1954   The Nobel Peace Prize is awarded to the Office of the UN High Commissioner for Refugees (UNHCR).

1956   Oct.: With Britain and France, Israel invades Egypt.
Nov.: UN Emergency Force moves into Sinai to keep the Israelis and Egyptians apart. It stays for eleven years.

1959   The UN Antarctic Treaty, prohibiting all military activity there, is signed.

1961   The UN General Assembly designates the 1960s as the First Development Decade.
Aug.: The Berlin Wall is built.
U Thant of Burma takes over as secretary-general of the UN.

1962   Oct.: U.S. spy planes detect Soviet missile sites in Cuba, causing the "Cuba crisis."

1963   A Nuclear Test Ban Treaty is signed, covering tests in the atmosphere, in outer space, and underwater.

1965	The Nobel Peace Prize is awarded to the United Nations International Children's Emergency Fund (UNICEF).
1967	A UN treaty bans the use of outer space as a base for weapons. The UN agrees to ban nuclear weapons in Latin America. June 5: The Six-Day War, between Israel and Syria, Jordan, and Egypt, starts. Nov.: The UN Security Council adopts a resolution outlining principles for lasting peace in the Middle East.
1968	A UN treaty on the nonproliferation of nuclear weapons aims to prevent the spread of nuclear weapons to more countries.
1969	The UN General Assembly designates the 1970s as the First Disarmament Decade.
1970	The UN General Assembly designates the 1970s as the Second Development Decade.
1971	A UN treaty bans the use of the seabed as a base for nuclear weapons.
1972	Kurt Waldheim of Austria becomes UN secretary-general.
1973	Oct.: The third Arab-Israeli War starts. The UN sets up a peace conference in Geneva and sends a second Emergency Force to Sinai.
1979	The UN General Assembly designates the 1980s as the Second Disarmament Decade.
1980	Sept.: The Iran/Iraq War starts.
1981	Jan. 1: The UN begins the Third Development Decade. The UNHCR is awarded the Nobel Peace Prize for the second time.
1982	Jan. 1: Javier Perez de Cuellar becomes UN secretary-general.
1985	The UN secretary-general intervenes personally to try to stop the Iran/Iraq War but is not successful. Mikhail Gorbachev becomes general secretary of the Soviet Union's Communist Party and effectively the Soviet leader. He introduces a new policy of open government and friendship with the West.
1986	The UN proclaims 1986 the International Year of Peace and the third Tuesday in September each year the International Day of Peace.
1988	A cease-fire is agreed between Iran and Iraq. The UN sends in observers. The UN peacekeeping forces are awarded the Nobel Peace Prize.
1989	Dec.: The Berlin Wall comes down, symbolizing the end of the Cold War.
1990	The Soviet Union begins to fall apart, splitting up into separate states. The United States is now the only world "superpower."
1991	Aug. 2: Iraq invades Kuwait and starts the Gulf War. The United States, with the backing of the UN, intervenes to defend Kuwait. Boutros Boutros-Ghali takes over as UN secretary-general. He is the first African to hold the post.
1992	The former state of Yugoslavia splits into separate states and fighting breaks out. A UN peacekeeping force is sent. A new famine is reported in Somalia. A UN relief operation is mounted, but the UN is criticized for inefficiency by other relief agencies.

Glossary

Biological weapon: A weapon that explodes and spreads the bacteria of disabling or fatal diseases.

Cash crop: A crop that is grown specifically for sale to another country, rather than for use by the local population.

Colony: A territory that is governed by another country.

Concentration camp: A guarded camp used to detain political prisoners and prisoners of war.

Conventional explosive: An explosive that makes use of chemical, not nuclear, energy.

Dysentery: An infectious disease that is spread by contaminated food and water. It can be fatal if not treated quickly.

Guerrilla: An unofficial soldier who is not normally linked to any government and is usually involved in independent acts of harassment and sabotage.

Human rights: Rights that are held to be belonging to any person. In 1948, the United Nations adopted the Universal Declaration of Human Rights. This details a number of economic, cultural, and political rights that every living person is entitled to. These rights include the right to life, liberty, education, freedom of movement, and equality before the law.

Immunization: Preventive treatment that protects the patient from a specific disease. The virus of a disease is usually injected into the patient to force the body to develop immunity to the disease.

Nuclear missiles: Weapons containing nuclear bombs that are fired from the ground. The destructive power of the bombs is created by the rapid release of nuclear energy.

Pesticide: A chemical that kills insects that are liable to damage crops.

Radiation sickness: An illness caused by exposure to *radioactivity*. The symptoms include nausea, vomiting, and hair loss. Death can occur six weeks or more after the exposure.

Radioactivity: High-speed and high-powered energy, which is released spontaneously from certain atoms, in the form of alpha, beta, or gamma rays. Nuclear explosions release large amounts of radioactivity.

Refugee: A person who seeks shelter in another country from war, persecution, or natural disaster.

Rehabilitation: Providing with the necessities of life, such as food, clothing, and shelter.

Resolution: A formal expression of an opinion or a statement of a decision that is put to, or adopted by, a meeting or legislative body.

Sanctions: Financial and military measures used by one or several states against another that has broken international law. The idea is to punish the country to force it to change its policy or policies.

Vaccination: The injection of a vaccine into a patient to protect against an infectious disease, such as smallpox, cholera, or diphtheria.

Further Information

If you would like to know more about the work of the United Nations and its agencies, contact the United Nations Information Center in your country.

Switzerland
United Nations Information Service
UN Office at Geneva
Palais des Nations
1211 Geneva 10
Switzerland

Phone (41 22) 734 6011

United Kingdom
United Nations Information Centre
20 Buckingham Gate
London
SW1E 6LB

Phone (44 71) 630 1981

United States of America
United Nations Information Center
1889 F Street N.W.
Washington, D.C. 20006
United States

Phone (202) 289-8670

Index